The Human Being and the Animal World

ROY WILKINSON

The publisher is grateful for the encouragement and support of Robert Dulaney in making this publication possible.

Originally published by Rudolf Steiner College Press.
This edition published by SteinerBooks.

Revised 1999

ISBN 978-0-945803-45-4

Printed in the United States of America

INTRODUCTION

It is the object of Steiner education to provide the children at every stage of their lives with what is needed for their inner development. At the age of ten they are beginning to feel the separation between their own individualities and the rest of the world. They want to learn about the outer world and to find their own relationship to it. They have an instinctive connection with the animal world. In studying this world in the way Dr. Steiner suggests, they will gain self-knowledge.

Up to the age of nine children do not differentiate clearly between their own inner life and the world outside. They experience the animals as brothers and sisters who can speak and act as human beings. Types of animals have been characterised in the fables which they have been told in their early years. Now the separation comes into self and the world. By showing animals in their relationship to the human being, the bridge is rebuilt and understanding fostered.

Human beings belong to nature and yet transcend it. They form a separate kingdom but at the same time this kingdom encompasses the others.

Young children are not ready for intellectual understanding but they have a feeling-understanding. They need explanations which can be appreciated in the emotional sense. In other words, the teacher must strive to produce lively and imaginative descriptions and characterisations. This is not a zoology period. Scientific explanations and details may be in place in the upper school from the age of sixteen onwards but for the moment pedagogical considerations are paramount rather than imparting knowledge. At ten, we can reckon with an instinctive understanding; at twelve, there will be the possibility of greater comprehension and the teacher should have in mind what will be taught in later years when the different fields of knowledge are brought together as, for instance, in the study of the human being at the age of fourteen.

As in other subjects, there are social and moral aspects to be taken into consideration and many points will arise which may well be elaborated in other lessons but, at this age, it would not be right to enter into discussion on ethics. However, by descriptions, attitudes, and manner of speaking, it may well be possible for the teacher to convey the fact that animals have rights, that they have the right to be respected in their instincts and in their place in their ecosystem, that they do not merely exist to be exploited.

The human being is at the centre of creation and all things should be taught in connection with this fact. Indeed, the animal world can only be understood in its relation to the human being. There is an interweaving and interdependence of everything in the world and when children realise this, they gain confidence and develop a social feeling. If they can understand the world and find their individual place in it, they may realise that they have responsibilities. If they can see that they owe their humanity to the animal creation, they may develop feelings of reverence and gratitude. If they can realise that human nature is able to overcome animal nature, an instinctive feeling for morality is implanted and this means an instinctive strengthening of the will forces.

This period in the Rudolf Steiner school, known as The Human Being and the Animal World, is one of the most difficult from the teachers' point of view. In the first place, they must subscribe to, or at least be in sympathy with, the ideas on evolution propounded by Dr. Steiner. (Otherwise, of course, they should not be in the school.) More than that, they must understand them and this understanding is not something that can be acquired the night before the lessons are given, nor is it something that can be superficially communicated.

The matter is also complicated by the fact that Dr. Steiner gave various indications to various people at various times and, although these are not contradictory, it is difficult to bring them into one cohesive whole.

Teachers have to acquire much information but should bear in mind the essential aim which is, in this case, to show the relationship between the human being and the animal in such a way that it becomes apparent that the human being is a compendium of the animal kingdom, alternatively expressed, that the animal kingdom is the human being spread out.

Many teachers, having gathered masses of information, feel that they must cover the subject comprehensively. It is a praiseworthy thought but enthusiasm sometimes has to be restricted. As with so many subjects, it is necessary to reduce the material to essentials, bearing in mind that the more intensive study follows in later years. Teachers must find the essence of what they want to say and put it over clearly and lucidly without getting lost in minor details, remembering also that time is limited. They must also, of course, be clear in their own minds as to why they are teaching this particular subject to that particular group.

It is not the purpose of this booklet to give the whole scientific-philosophical background to the subject. This must be sought in the recommended literature, but it is to be hoped that these few practical indications will be useful.

RUDOLF STEINER'S IDEAS ON EVOLUTION

Contrary to the Darwinistic ideas of the human being as the final product of animal evolution, Dr. Steiner considers animals to be the by-products of human development. The human being has been involved from the beginning but not in a physical form. The human being existed spiritually and the animal forms represent physically incarnated soul forces which the human being had to dispense with in order to mature sufficiently to receive the ego. A certain harmony had to be established. As in life—assuming that we are trying to progress in the betterment of ourselves—we are trying to overcome the lower passions to evolve to something higher, so throughout evolution, the passions were separated out from humans and these were incorporated as animals.

Let us start from the point that the gods, or the divine spiritual beings, decided to create the world and humanity. For this we have a good authority in the first chapter of the first book of the Bible.

Before the world came into being materially, it existed under different conditions. Immediately previous to the material, there was a "watery" state; before that an "airy- gaseous"; and before that something akin to "warmth". (These expressions are put in inverted commas because the terms are only approximate. The warmth, water, air-gas were not the physical elements we know today).

Into the original "warmth" element the gods poured something of their own substance, thus forming the basis of what later became the human physical body. At this stage it was not material. A transformation of this "body" took place during the next "airy-gaseous" epoch when other spiritual beings added their contribution. A third change took place during the "'watery" period and other qualities were added. Then comes a time for a fourth development when material physical substance will appear. Before this we have to think of non-material existence in the same sense as we can think of the human soul as having a spiritual existence when not incarnated in the body.

A result of this fourfold development are the four kingdoms of nature as we know them today: mineral, plant, animal, and human.

The fourth era can be subdivided into various epochs named by Dr. Steiner the Polaric, Hyperborean, Lemurian, Atlantean, and Post-Atlantean, which brings us up to date.

These periods are comparable with those of geological science. The Polaric and Hyperborean epochs are contemporary with the Azoic era of geology, that is, the early period from which no organic remains can be traced. The human being was not incarnated. The chart shows how the later periods, from Lemuria onwards, can be compared with the normally accepted development. There is no conflict of opinion on the order in which the animals appear but anthroposophical thought does not accept the physical development of one species from another. Each species was a new creation and spiritual beings were the creators.

Era	Epoch	Animal Development	Developments according to Rudolf Steiner	
			the Human Being	*Earth*
Paleozoic	Cambrian Ordovician Silurian	Invertebrates Lower forms of life (water)	The human being exists in spirit form	Lemuria Geological formations begin
	Devonian Carboniferous Permian	Shellfish, Insects First amphibians and Reptiles, Fish	The human being incarnates into a still plastic body	Mid-Lemuria
Mesozoic	Triassic Jurassic Cretaceous	Age of reptiles, Saurians Beginning of mammals and birds		
Cenozoic	Tertiary	Mammals	The human being takes on a firmer body	Atlantis
	Quaternary (Pleistocene) (Holocene)		The human being in physical body	Post-Atlantis

The development of the earth during these periods was towards material densification and the progress of living things went parallel with it. Although we speak of the human being, it might be more exact to speak of human-substance or human-essence since what we call the human being today is a being endowed with the ego (the individual self-directing principle) but it was only during the process of earth evolution, i.e. through the Polaric, Hyperborean, etc. epochs that he or she has become capable of receiving this, as a further gift of the gods. It should also be borne in mind that there are spiritual beings of negation and therefore development is not straightforward.

At the beginning of earth evolution (the fourth development beginning with the Polaric epoch) this human-essence only existed in a spiritual form. It contained life forces (forces of growth) and soul or astral forces (lusts, passions, desires) in chaotic abundance. The gods were active in it. It was the object of the gods to create an independent being. For this purpose the human being had to receive a godlike quality, the ego. To receive the ego, the substance had to be modified and the modification or purification consisted of casting out a superfluity of undesirable elements. As the earth progressed towards physical existence, i.e. materialisation, these forces were discarded by the potential human being. These portions of the astral then took on the physical forms appropriate to the ruling conditions of the earth at that time and these forms are the ancestors of our present animals. Where conditions become impossible for that form of life, they died out, hence the prehistoric monsters. The individual animal forms are therefore hardened single portions of the human being and are a manifestation of an astral force or forces.

One cannot be dogmatic in categorizing. Evolution has been a long process with many by-ways and there are mixed ingredients. However, by way of example, we can think of the rapacity of a lion, also its courage. We think of stubbornness in a bull, interspersed with choleric episodes. The pig is a gourmand.

The human being remained in spiritual existence until sufficiently mature and until a suitable physical body was available. This is the reason why there are no bones of prehistoric humans to be found along with those of prehistoric animals. The human being was there, but in spirit.

We see then that humanity is not the result of animal evolution but at the beginning of it and central to it, indeed the cause of it. The animal world represents soul qualities which the human being has discarded although still retaining remnants of them. Some of our common expressions bear witness to the fact that we recognise soul qualities in the animal related to our own: to act the goat, lion-hearted, wolf it down, cunning as a fox.

There is a further consideration in the matter of the physical organism. The human being has achieved a balance and a harmony in his or her organs. The animal is one-sided. If we could imagine all animal organisms combined, we have the framework of the human being, brought of course to a higher stage of development. Alternatively, we could say that single components of the human organism are independent and manifest themselves in the animal world.

THE HUMAN BEING AND ANIMAL COMPARED

Since the animal is specialised in one direction, it is only to be expected that its ability in that particular sphere is greater than that of the human being.

The front leg of a mole is a great instrument for digging—much better than the human hand. Weight for weight, a mole can move twelve times more material in a given time than a miner with pickaxe and shovel. The claw of a tiger is much more efficient than human hands at holding prey; the teeth of the rodent continually renew themselves. In certain matters, therefore, the animal is more perfect than the human being; but this perfection is also its limitation. The animal acts out of organic necessity. It can do no other. It does not possess a thinking intelligence but is endowed with a natural, or supernatural intelligence which directs it.

To understand the animal it is necessary to look first at the structure of the human being and then for an exaggeration of some feature in the animal. Which part of the human body is represented in this animal? Then ask: Which part of the animal has been developed at the expense of the rest? Some answers are obvious. The cow has its digestive system; the elephant the extraordinary transformation of nose and upper lip into its trunk.

In the human being there is a balance. Nothing has been pushed to its limit but the fact of the withholding of forces means that he or she has other possibilities. These are in the nature of inner, soul, development. In some respects human beings are less perfect than animals but they have the possibility of advancing. The animal impulses still live in the human being but as humans we struggle against the animal nature—at least we do if we have any pretensions to morality.

The existence of different types of teeth show how the human being is balanced. The ruminants have exceptional molars; the predatory animals, canine teeth; the rodents, incisors. In the human jaw these are all present but harmoniously balanced.

The animal becomes independent soon after birth. The child does not. The animal lives eternally in the present; the human being in the past, present and future. The animal is limited, circumscribed, fated; the human being has infinite possibilities. The animal's limbs or its organs are its tools; the human hand is not a tool in this sense but his brain can fashion tools. The animal's legs are to carry its body. Human beings have a different leg and foot development. They only need two legs to stand and these are differently constructed from those of the animal giving them the possibility of the upright position and the freedom to use their hands. The animals' paws serve their own needs. Human hands serve humanity and the world. They are a manifestation of freedom.

The animal and its surroundings are one. Where the environment becomes unsuitable, the animal dies out. The animal is equipped for its surroundings. Human beings create their own.

The animal head is an extension of the spine. The human head sits above it and moves freely. The eyes look out into the world, not to the earth. The animal makes noises dependent on its needs. The human being can speak or be silent, choose a theme and discuss it.

THE GROUP SOUL

In the case of a human being we shall speak of a biography. In the animal kingdom we can only speak of the story of the species. Human beings will behave individually. They can be angels or beasts, even as Mephistopheles says—using their powers to be more beastly than the beast—but an animal, although it may have individual characteristics, is always an animal. A cat is always a cat.

The higher principle of individuality, the ego, has entered the human being so that we consider each person an individual in his own right. This is not the case with the animal. Each animal is not an individual in the same sense as the human but each species has its individuality, its ego, or its group soul. This is to be thought of as something quite real but existing only in a spiritual form. The group soul is, so to speak, the guiding principle of the whole species, It is the equivalent of the ego in the human being. Each individual member of the species is connected with and directed by the group soul along some mysterious, invisible path. A rough analogy would be to think of the human fingers directed and coordinated by the human spirit. In some ways the group soul has much greater intelligence than the human being does. Think of all the wonderful things an animal does, as we say, by instinct—the mole in its burrow, the bird building its nest, the badger with its sett and number of escape holes. Think, too, of a collection of bees as the physical expression of a beehive spiritual being.

We speak of an intelligent animal. We might say that the animal does not use its intelligence. It is the intelligence, the cosmic wisdom through the group soul that uses the animal. This wisdom is incorporated in its organism. The animal acts in a certain way because it cannot do otherwise.

Human beings have all the possibilities inherent in the animal but they can direct them in their own way by means of the individualised intelligence. In the animal, what is experienced goes straight into deed. There is no reflection. It reacts immediately. It neither decides nor declines.

CLASSROOM WORK

Teachers with orderly minds will want to classify each animal in accordance with the principles explained. Unfortunately the world of nature does not allow itself to be so neatly divided into sections and subsections. It is difficult to set up an exact schedule for the simple reason that evolution has been going on for a long time and the path has deviations. Practically, therefore, some animals represent transitional forms, some are mixtures and many can be looked upon in more ways than one. For our purpose, then, we must find the most striking examples.

Insofar as teachers of this age group (10/11) are not called upon to give a course on zoology, they can consider themselves lucky. The capacity of children of this age is also not too great. Obviously the greater the teachers' knowledge and understanding, the better will they be able to handle the material but detail is not required. This can come in the upper school. It is sufficient at this stage to grasp the principles and convey the essentials, i.e., that animals have one particular organ or faculty further developed than that of the human, and in this one-sided development they have achieved greater perfection, but their progress ends there. The human being has held back certain forces and hence has the possibility of further development. The animal world is man spread out. Man is a synthesis of the animal kingdom at a higher level.

Teachers do not have to say this in so many words. They convey it, without explanations, through their descriptions. Where they touch on moral topics, they must be particularly careful not to point the moral. Let the imaginative picture or description work by itself.

In the timetable, one period of The Human Being and the Animal World of three to four weeks (main lesson of two hours daily) is envisaged for Class 4 (age 10) and a further period the following year. However, the teacher should have in mind the whole sequence of studies for the next few years. There are The Human Being and the Animal World periods in this class and the next. In Class 5 comes also Plant Study, with possibly one or two periods, then Geology and a study of Minerals in Class 6. Also in Class 6 there is a beginning of a study of Physics, Chemistry and Mechanics which are continued into Class 8. There should then be a study of "man", taking into consideration all these matters dealt with in the meantime and showing their connection with the human being.

The first period should be fairly simple and the first few days should be spent in considering the human being himself and the significance of the limbs. By way of making this clear, Dr. Steiner suggests describing and comparing the cuttlefish and the mouse with the human being. The point of this will be obvious on reading the following.

THE THREEFOLD HUMAN BEING

There will be no shortage of specimens of homo sapiens in the class so observation should be easy The children themselves will have lots to say but their thoughts should be led along these lines:

If we look at the structure of the human being, at the outer form, we see immediately three main parts: the head, the trunk, and the limbs.

The head is spherical like the earth. The outer part is hard like the earth's crust. In the head are eyes with which to see, ears for hearing, a nose for smelling and a mouth for tasting. The mouth is also used for speaking. Through the head we get impressions and learn about the world; but the head rests, and is only carried about on the rest of the body. It sits there on the top of the human frame like a watchtower, looking around into the world and grabbing all the information it can pick up.

If we look at the limbs of the human being, we see that they are active. They do things. The forelimbs, which we call arms, do not have to share in carrying the weight of the body as is the case with the animals. The arms are free. They can do good things; they can also do bad but having a choice is part of being a human. Think of all the things that hands can do—build, write, play the piano, and so on. The feet and legs are so well constructed that the body can be carried upright. The feet carry us from place to place.

The head is round. The hard part is on the outside and the soft part inside. The limbs in themselves are not round, indeed they seem to be stuck into the body but if we stretch out, we find ourselves standing within a circle and the limbs are like radii. In legs and arms the hard part is inside and the soft out.

Between head and limbs is the trunk—of which the upper part, the chest, is also round and below it are stomach and intestines. The chest consists of a bony sort of cage, not solid like the head but with bone and space alternating. The bones are known as the ribs and there is a special arrangement whereby the chest can expand and contract. In the chest are heart and lungs, the rhythmic system.

Food and air enter the body via the head but it is the trunk which is the workshop. The air comes into the lungs where it refreshes the blood; the food comes into the stomach where it is digested and transformed so that it can be used by other parts of the body.

The head rests quietly. The limbs are active. The rhythmic system is something in between. For the most part we are not aware of our breathing but we can bring it to consciousness when we will.

Having given some picture of the human being in the threefold aspect we now turn to consider the form of other animals. Although Dr. Steiner suggests the cuttlefish and mouse, there is no reason why the teacher should not deal with other related animals if he so wishes. The octopus or squid would answer the purpose equally well and any other member of the rodent family.

The matter should be put to the children somewhat in this fashion (Pictures may be necessary):

We are now going to study an animal that probably very few of you have ever seen. It is called the cuttlefish but it is not a fish at all, although it lives in the sea. It has an oval, slightly flat shape and it is about 18 inches long. It has fins down the side of its body and a beak almost like a bird. The surroundings of its mouth are drawn out into eight snake-like arms which are continually waving about, stretching, moving, as if they wanted to feel what was in the neighbourhood. Besides these arms, the cuttlefish has two long feelers, called tentacles, which stretch out even further and have suckers on their ends. It has big eyes which look very much awake.

The cuttlefish can move in various ways. By waggling its fins it can swim. It can turn itself on end and walk along the bed of the ocean on its arms. It also has another very special way of moving. It can suck water in and blow it out quickly so that it travels backwards by jet propulsion.

It has poisonous spittle glands and a little sack full of ink which it can squirt out if it wants to escape from an enemy. This ink is the basis of the "sepia" that painters use. It is a dark brown colour. The intestines and all those things equivalent to what we have in our trunk are very simple.

Let us imagine a cuttlefish lying in the water. We see it lying there horizontally, gently moving its fins to keep its balance. Its arms and tentacles are gently moving to and fro. Its back appears to be orange, its arms green and its fins are a transparent violet,

Suddenly a little fish comes near. The cuttlefish gets excited. It does not tremble as we do but its colours change. There are now patches of red and brown on its back; its eyes reflect pink, blue and green. For the moment its arms may be curled up but then like lightning they shoot out and grab the prey. The suckers hold the victim tight. Then perhaps something frightens the cuttlefish. It squirts out its ink and hurries off in the confusion.

We see then that the cuttlefish has really no legs and very little of what would be our trunk. It finds out all that is going on in the world around it by means of its arms and tentacles. These are like its eyes and ears and nose. The human being perceives what is taking place in the world through senses which are located in the head. So we could say that the cuttlefish is like a head that has decided to go off into the world alone. In this case it is a watery world so the cuttlefish is a sort of swimming head.

The mouse is an animal that we all know. Its shape is quite different from that of the cuttlefish. It is a tiny animal and if we only get a quick glance at it as it scurries across the room, we scarcely see either head or legs, but only a trunk with a tail, and possibly little ears sticking up. If we can get a closer look, we see that it has a small, pointed snout, bright eyes, whiskers and, like all its relations, special teeth. It is an animal which gnaws, that is, it uses its teeth as tools and these teeth, unlike ours, keep renewing themselves. The mouse has a sort of soft, smooth fur. Its hind feet are a little larger than the front ones and this means it can also jump. The tail is covered with scales.

We note particularly that the mouse seems to be all trunk. The pointed head is only an extension of it; the legs are tiny by comparison.

Suppose we are sitting quietly in a room but we know that a mousehole is near. Suddenly we see a little face in the hole, then it has gone. It reappears, disappears again. A mouse comes out a few feet, stops, looks round, seems to take one dive and disappears down its hole again. It comes again, scurries across the floor, stops, sits up, looks around, hurries off. Next time it finds a piece of bread and as we are very quiet, it sits up, balancing itself with its tail stretched behind it, takes the meal in its forepaws and eats. There is a slight noise and it is gone. The mouse is a quick, nervous, little creature. In its bodily form it is all trunk.

The cuttlefish has no limbs, no ears, no snout but it is equipped otherwise for its way of life. An animal like the mouse, however, needs these appendages as servants for its trunk.

We are comparing the form of the human being with the form of the animal and we see that the cuttlefish is like a human head; the mouse resembles the human being in the trunk. Now we come to the limbs. We have seen a "head" animal and a "trunk" animal. Where is there a "limb" animal?

There will be many suggestions all of which the teacher will have to refute for the simple reason that, from this point of view, there is not one.

The fact is that there is no animal which resembles the human being in the limb system. The monkey may come nearest but the monkey's hand does not grasp like that of the human neither do its feet touch the ground in the same way. The monkey also goes for the most part on all fours.

Let us now look a little closer at the limbs. We will compare the human hand with the paw of an animal.

By comparison we can see that the paw is a tool for some specific purpose but we cannot say that about the hand. Wonderful, versatile, flexible, useful though it may be, it is not immediately apparent that the hand call do anything special. Compare it, for instance, with the forepaw of a mole—what a poor shovel the hand is; but the hand can use a shovel which the mind behind it has invented. That is the difference. The wing of a bird is wonderful in its construction. The fish has fins to drive itself along, but the human being can make wings for an aeroplane and wheels for cars and propellors for ships. Thus we see that the human hand is less perfect in some respects than the corresponding limb of an animal, but we also see that it has more possibilities.

Besides handling tools, the human being uses his hands in other ways. He shakes hands with his fellows as a sign of friendship and greeting. Hands are clasped together in prayer. Some people have the power of healing by the laying on of hands. Hands can also be destructive as well as creative and that is important for the whole earth. No single hand is like another.

It is not necessary to express the following in words. The pictures will suffice in the child's mind at this stage. Nevertheless the teacher should have these thoughts in the back of his or her mind and convey what is possible without being pedantic.

The animal has no reasoning power with which to make tools and an animal with hands like a human being would be a failure. The animal is concerned with getting the means for its existence and that is its life, conditioned by its organism. Human life extends beyond the struggle for existence. Men and women create, and the hand is the tool of the human spirit. This contrast of hand and paw is a picture of human freedom and animal bondage.

If we compare the feet and legs of a human being with the feet and hind legs of the animal, we again see a difference. The human foot is unique in its construction. It has a forepart, a heel, and an arch in between. Human walking is also unique. Only the human being has contact with the earth in a threefold way—raising the heel, carrying the foot forward and setting it down again in rhythmical progression. The leg, too, is different, with muscles to aid this walking. The upright position is possible when feet and legs are constructed in this way.

At this point it is perhaps a good idea to let the children name a whole range of animals and compare them with the human being. It gives a splendid opportunity for class participation, for stimulating both feeling and will. It will arouse lively interest and also give opportunity for reflection. It provides good practice in observing and describing. The teacher will then pick out the salient points and repeat them or point out what has been missed. There will be no shortage of suggestions. At some point the teacher might explain that, although no animals have limbs comparable with those of the human being, they possess limbs nevertheless and these might be very special.

These are the important matters as far as we are concerned at present:

> Animals are one-sided developments.
>
> The human being is balanced.
>
> Animals of the same species act like one another.
>
> The animals' limbs are their tools. Even the head is a tool.
>
> The human hand is not a tool but it can make implements to serve him.
>
> Animals can do some things better than human beings can, but the latter can do everything that an animal can.
>
> The human being goes upright and has an individual facial expression.
>
> The animal goes on all fours with its head towards the ground and has no distinctive individual facial features.
>
> Men and women have hands.

Perhaps during the discussion, or on some suitable occasion, the other aspect which we mentioned in the introduction, i.e., that each animal species also represents a soul quality, could be broached. This aspect can be approached by getting the children to think of similes where animals are introduced:

As clumsy as an elephant

As cunning as a fox

As timid as a mouse

As busy as a bee

As fat as a pig, etc.

At the end of this discussion the teacher can:

1. Repeat such matters as reinforce the view of the importance of hands.

2. Extract certain points as a lead to the next chapter which is: to see which part of the human organism is manifested in exaggerated form in the animal. At the same time to see which part of the animal has been developed at the expense of the rest.

The following are factual descriptions. The author has not attempted to put matters in the artistic form in which they should be presented to the children in addition to facts. It is also helpful to create imaginatively an actual situation. The following few sentences give an indication of what is required and the verses may help but the teacher is recommended to fire his or her own imagination.

"Down on the farm it was milking time. Across the field a herd of cows was making its way to the milking shed. Each animal was moving forward at a slow unhurried pace. It seemed an effort each time for them to pick up a foot and put it forward. Heads bobbed up and down slowly as the animals slouched along—and so forth."

THE COW

Heavily, wearily, moves the cow
In the peaceful country scene,
Sleepily nodding towards the ground
As she grazes the pastures green.

Her big, bulky mass of a body
Flops on the earth and she seems,
Chewing and chewing and chewing,
Lost in her own world of dreams.

In England the cow is one of our most common animals. We see her everywhere in the fields. Her produce—milk, butter and cheese—comes into almost every home. A group of cows lying contentedly in a field in the warm sunshine, chewing the cud, presents a delightful picture of peace and tranquillity. The cow cannot be hurried. To see a cow running is to see something quite out of place. Her movements are naturally slow and very different from those of the horse. She is not built for speed. She has a large, heavy head, a massive body and relatively thin legs. She has a dreamy look in her eyes, and no wonder—for her chief occupation is eating and digesting. When we humans have had a big meal and our stomachs are full, we also feel sleepy, but what if we had four stomachs like the cow! With her, sleepiness or dreaminess is a permanent condition. The human being takes in about 1/40 of his own weight in nourishment daily but the cow needs 1/8. We can see how the cow is adapted to chewing by her long jaw and if we could see inside her mouth we should see huge back teeth. Inside the bulky body there are the four stomachs and the intestines which are 22 times as long as the animal's body. The cow has a heart and lungs and other organs but her digestive system takes pride of place. The cow does not chew her food and then swallow it but she first swallows it and then brings it up again to chew. This is what is known as chewing the cud and the animals which eat in this way are known as ruminants. When we see cows lying so peacefully in the fields, they are really working hard—digesting.

One result of this process is the production of milk which is so useful in human nourishment. The other is the excellent manure which nourishes the soil.

We can also judge the nature of the cow by the sound she makes, the "moo". It is a thick, heavy, earthy sound.

The cow then, could be described as a walking stomach.

THE HORSE

Dancing on tip-toes,

This is the horse,

Scarcely touching the ground.

Tossing his mane,

Flicking his tail,

Rearing and jumping around.

See him prancing

Over the field,

Kicking his hooves in the air,

Bucking, rolling,

Galloping swiftly,

Unburdened of every care.

The horse presents a great contrast to the cow. The head is more erect, the eye more lively, the body more round. Under the sleek skin one can see the muscles rippling. Whereas the cow has a cloven hoof which helps her to stand around in the mud, the horse has a consolidated hard hoof more suited to running over the ground. The hoof is something very special. It is a sort of collar round the central bone and it combines firmness with a certain elasticity. As it gets worn away it replenishes itself.

The horse has a beautiful mane which it tosses when it feels frisky, and a tail which consists of long strands of hair, in contrast to the cow's tail which is a bony structure.

If we look at a cow and a horse side by side, we could almost imagine the cow sinking into the earth but the horse is rising above it. In legends we have heard of a winged horse, but we have never heard of a winged cow. If a cow belongs to the element of earth, then we could say that the horse belongs to the air. The open field or the prairie is its proper environment.

The horse is sensitive and nervous and if we observe closely we see a slight tremor passing over it from time to time. This sort of sensitivity is also apparent when it neighs, making a nervous sort of sound. When it neighs, it also shivers. This sensitivity shows itself in other ways for in its nature it combines many qualities. It can be patient but also impatient, slow or quick, good-tempered or angry. Its really wild nature has been tamed by humans for their own use. Because of its build, its intelligence and its special features, the horse is closely connected with the human being. Its centre of gravity is just right for the saddle; its shape and its rhythmical movement make it easy to ride. In fact the horse has several rhythms. It can walk and we count 1, 2, 3, 4. It can trot with a sort of "clippetyclop" and it can also gallop. The horse easily understands what its master or mistress wants and has served in many capacities—for riding, for pulling carts, for work in the fields. The old Teutonic warriors felt so close to their horses that the animals had to be buried with them.

In spite of its large size, the horse is graceful and if we tried to say why, we could not say that it is on account of its shape, but on account of its movement.

In its structure the horse has one great speciality and this really shows how it is connected to the earth and the air. If we compare its feet with the feet and hands of the human being, we see that the horse goes on very extended middle fingers and middle toes. In actual fact it touches the ground very lightly. We could look upon the horse as a dancer, a ballet dancer even. Its physical speciality is the long middle finger and toe.

THE ELEPHANT

If a friend knocks into us or treads on our toes, what do we say? "You clumsy elephant". Clumsy, that is the impression that the elephant makes on us but it is only partly true.

The elephant is our largest living quadruped and, although most of us have not seen it in its natural surroundings, we have seen one in a zoo. It has a massive, unshaped body, supported on four huge pillars for legs, soft soles on its feet and a soft tread. Its head merges with its body and it has no neck to speak of. In its head it has comparatively tiny eyes and it has large or medium sized ears according to whether it is an African or Indian type. At one end of its huge body it has a ridiculously small tail but at the other, its pride and glory, that wonderful instrument known as the trunk. On each side of the trunk are the tusks which grow forward. If we could look into the elephant's mouth we should see only one big tooth in each jaw but these teeth are also remarkable. The human child changes teeth at about the age of six but the elephant goes on changing teeth all its life. These teeth replenish themselves six times over.

In colour the elephant is usually grey or greyish brown. Its skin is thick and has folds in it. Bothersome bloodsucking insects get into these folds but the elephant has friends. These are the birds who sit on its back and pick out the tormentors.

One could hardly speak of an elephant walking. It plods or ambles and has a peculiar gait in that it moves foreleg and backleg on the same side together. It will climb a mountain by bending its forelegs and going up, so to speak, on its elbows. Coming down, if the hill is steep, it will slide half-sitting.

The elephant stands anything from ten to fifteen feet high and weighs two or three tons. It eats two or three hundred pounds of food a day and drinks 40 gallons of water. Pregnancy in an elephant lasts for about 20 months. When the baby is born, it is about three feet tall and it can get up and run about only a few hours after birth. It needs eight or ten years to grow up and it achieves maturity at about the age of 20. The tusks begin to grow in the second year. Mothers usually have a single calf and they are very devoted, looking after their children for many years. Elephants live to be about 60 or 70.

Although such a strong, massive creature, the elephant is very sensitive. It sleeps little and is very aware of sounds and smells around it. A mouse can frighten it. Some people say it can smell food or water six miles away. By nature it is a peaceful animal. It is a vegetarian and does not attack other animals. It is persevering and, in its own way, gentle.

The elephant is at home in Africa and India. It can live in all sorts of surroundings. It lives in bushy, wooded country, on high mountains or in steamy jungles. It is a wise and intelligent animal and can be put to work for human needs. It is useful in hauling timber. It is said that "an elephant never forgets". In former times elephants were trained for war. A famous general, Hannibal, once tried to cross the Alps with elephants to attack the Romans.

Elephants like to live in herds of anywhere from 10 to 50 but the herd is really one big family—mothers, fathers, uncles, cousins. The leader of the herd is usually a female and when the herd wanders, she leads. The little ones follow in line, and the males, the bulls, bring up the rear. Sometimes it happens that a tame elephant escapes. Then it has a very unpleasant time because, if it cannot find its family, it has to live alone since no other herd will accept it. Then it becomes angry and can be dangerous. It is then known as a "rogue" elephant.

Elephants like water and they have great fun frisking about in mud and water. They squirt themselves and one another. They can swim across rivers or even walk across with their trunks stuck out like snorkels. They are also wanderers and may travel five or six miles in a night. Usually they keep to regular paths.

A mealtime in the elephant family is a noisy affair. There is a snapping and a crashing of branches as the animals pull them down. There is the sound of the crushing of twigs as their great teeth chew them up. One elephant might be ripping up the ground with his tusks in search of something to eat. There is a snorting and a blowing and a chomping, and a sucking sound as heavy feet are drawn out of the mud.

Elephants have been hunted in the past for the ivory of their tusks. Now they are getting scarce but reserved areas have been made in Africa where they can live in peace.

The elephant's speciality is obviously its trunk. It seems as if all the rest of the animal has been neglected in order that upper lip and nose could be specially developed. There has also been a modification in tooth formation. The tusks are transformed teeth and they grow longer all through life. The trunk is like a fifth limb and it is wonderful what can be done with it. The trunk collects leaves, twigs, food of all sorts and stuffs it in the mouth. The mouth cannot feed; it has to be fed. The trunk is also used for drinking. Water is squirted into the mouth. The trunk is so sensitive that it can pick up a coin or a piece of paper. It can pick up a log or pick up a man and put him in the driver's position. In Basel zoo there used to be an elephant who could play the mouth organ. The trunk is also used for caressing a sweetheart.

We said that the elephant has small eyes. With its wonderful trunk perhaps it does not need to see very well. If we watch an elephant, we see his trunk is continually wandering about, sniffing and probing everything that it senses around it. Perhaps the trunk discovers everything. It is a tool, a weapon, but also a sort of eye, ear and hand.

THE LION

With his magnificent head and mane, his proud eye and his majestic movements, the lion is truly called the "King of Beasts". The lioness, although less spectacular in appearance, also has a regal presence.

Let us compare the bodily structure of lions with that of the animals already studied. The elephant is all bulk; the cow is angular; the horse round; the lion's body is slim and streamlined. The elephant has massive legs; the cow, bony; the horse, delicate; but the legs of the lion are muscular. The lion, and all members of the cat family, can stretch out a paw. They have claws at the end, which they can extend or withdraw, and a padded foot. The legs have a tremendous mobility and are for leaping and springing; also for gliding along and crouching.

The lion lives in the grassy plains of South Africa, although their spread used to be much wider. They hunt for a living. Unlike some of the animals we have considered such as cows, horses, and elephants, lions are meat eaters. Their teeth, jaws, and mouths demonstrate this aspect. When lions roar, the rest of creation trembles. They can run for miles without getting tired.

What is it that is special in lions? We can see from their build and movements that it is the chest system, and that which is within it, that is highly developed. Like all the cat family, it has a well developed rhythmic system. The lion has a mighty heart and mighty lungs.

THE CAMEL

To us the camel seems a very peculiar animal but to those people living in desert areas it is extremely useful. In fact it is the camel that makes life possible there. With its two humps, its arched neck, its long legs and its strangely shaped body, the camel is very strange in appearance. (A near relative, the dromedary, has one hump). It has long hair on its chest, on the upper parts of its legs and on the humps. It has big feet, a short tail and a look of disdain on its face. The upper lip is split and overhangs the mouth. It has long eyelashes and can close its nostrils. It has the same gait as the elephant which makes it an uncomfortable animal to ride. It is a stubborn creature and only gives way after making a fuss. It is nervous of other animals and is easily disturbed by them. It can be dangerous if it gets cross. It seems to live in its own world, indifferent to almost everything and everybody. The impression it gives is really grotesque.

Yet the camel is a wonderful animal in its own way. Many people have cause to be grateful to it, particularly in hot arid areas where no other animals could survive. It has been used as a pack animal for crossing the deserts for thousands of years and it is known as "the ship of the desert". It produces milk and a sort of wool. Even its dung is useful as there is no wood in the desert and the dung can be dried and used as fuel. When a sandstorm blows up, the camel lies down and its owner gets beside it for protection. At night, when it is cold, the camel keeps him warm. This animal is at home in a dry climate. With regard to food, it is quite extraordinary. It is a vegetarian and a ruminant but it can get along on any bits of leaves or twigs that it can find. Even thorny bushes are welcome. It eats everything up, thorns as well. If it finds sufficient green leaves it can even go without water. In any case it can go for several days without drinking. When it has been travelling and is getting thirsty, it is almost uncontrollable as soon as it scents water, which may be a mile away.

The distinctive feature of the camel is of course its humps. These are nothing more than mounds of fat and can weigh up to 30 pounds. In days of plenty, the hump grows big and when there is not much to eat, then the camel lives off its own fat which it carries on its back. Then the humps can sag until they are scarcely noticeable.

If the cow is a walking stomach, then the camel is a living larder. It is the only animal to carry its own storehouse with it.

THE DOG

The dog, like the horse, is a very close friend of humans. Its ancestors were probably wolves and in the natural state they are wild, ferocious and greedy; but under the influence of the human being the dog has become a faithful servant. It is used as a guard for our homes, as a helper on the farm. Some dogs are very specially trained to guide the blind. The dog is one of the domestic animals that we take into our homes like the cat. The latter is a close relative of the lion and has the same rhythmic quality but in our homes it has become gentle.

Let us look at some of the differences between dog and cat. The dog has longer legs and they are not so muscular. The dog is a runner and not a jumper. It cannot climb and it cannot retract its claws. Instead of lying in wait for its prey or stalking it and then pouncing like the cat, the dog runs it down. In comparison with the dainty ways of a cat, the dog is tough, crude and boisterous.

When we observe the head of a dog, we see a long pointed snout and when we see a dog approach something unknown, we notice how it stretches out its snout and sniffs suspiciously. When a stranger comes, it barks or even bites. Why? Because it is afraid. This tells us about the nature of the dog. Its nerve system and certain senses are highly developed. That is why a dog can follow a trail by scent, why it can be trained to lead the blind, to act as a watchdog or round up sheep.

BIRDS AND FISHES

The teacher is reminded to use poetic descriptions and to instance actual or imaginative situations.

So far we have talked about land animals, mammals, which bring their young alive into the world and suckle them. These are the animals which are nearest to the human being but we will now study two others which belong to quite different elements: the fish and the bird. Both of these lay eggs but they are hatched out under quite different circumstances.

As the bird belongs to the air, so the fish belongs to the water. As the air carries the bird, so the water carries the fish, but the fish dies if it is brought to land.

Two thirds of the surface of the globe are covered by that restless, moving element which we call water, and in all this water—oceans, rivers, and lakes—live fish. They, too, are always in movement.

In the ever-flowing water
Up and down I love to roam,
Whether it be lake or river
Water, water is my home.

Perhaps a glimpse of me you saw,
In the water something shone.
You looked again, what did you see?
Nothing, I had gone.

Some fish live in deep water, some in shallow, some in fresh water and some in salt. Some alternate between fresh and salt. There are fish that travel thousands of miles across the ocean and they move in shoals of thousands and thousands. When a fish lays eggs, it does not lay five or six like a blackbird or sparrow, but it may lay five hundred or a few million.

These things tell us something very special about the fish, and that is that the fish race possesses an extraordinary life force.

There are some 13,000 known species of fish roaming around in the waters of the world. Some have very fancy arrangements of fins and some are fairly straightforward. Some gleam with a silver sheen and others are found in all colours of the rainbow, particularly those in the tropics.

All fish have bony or cartilaginous skeletons consisting of a spine and ribs. At one end of the spine is the head and at the other the tail. They have no real limbs but are endowed with fins with which they can propel themselves and keep their balance. They are covered with scales which overlap one another like shingles on a roof and they always feel slimy to the touch.

In movement a fish is very quick. It can flash by, up, down, turn this way or that, twisting its whole body very quickly. The fish has nostrils but it only uses them for smelling. It does not breathe air but takes water into its mouth and forces it out again through its gills. By this process oxygen is extracted from the water that goes into the blood stream to keep it healthy.

The fish has big eyes but no real ears. However, there is a sensitive line all round its body through which it feels vibrations.

It is very different from other animals in that its eggs are laid on the ocean or river bed and then left to take care of themselves. No wonder we borrow a phrase from the fish world and describe a person as "cold-blooded". However, nature takes care of things and sees that plenty are hatched out.

If we study the structure of a fish, we can say that there is just barely a threefoldness—head, trunk and tail—but the head is only one end of the trunk and the tail the other. They are all very closely connected. There is no real head system, chest system and limbs. Looking at the fish in comparison with the human being, we can say that it is all trunk, but trunk adapted to the element in which it lives.

Shelley was quite right when he said in his poem to the skylark: "Hail to thee, blithe spirit", and later when he compared the lark to "an unbodied joy".

A spirit is something definitely not material and joy without a body is even further away from substance.

Although birds must come down to earth, it is the air that is their real environment. They are built for flying. A bird can travel through the air at 50 miles per hour—a swallow even faster. Birds' bones are hollow. Their lungs have air pockets which extend beyond the lungs and when a bird breathes in, the air goes not only into the lungs but into these air pockets and from there into the hollow bones. We have only to watch seagulls flying over the cliffs to see how the air is the element of the birds.

We can also think of the way in which animals express themselves. The cow moos, the lion roars, the horse neighs, but the bird "sings". This singing is really a whistling and has nothing to do with a voice but purely with an air stream being formed. The birds' song is not an earthy sound like that of other animals.

What is the outstanding feature of a bird besides the fact that it can fly? Its feathers. The feathers in themselves are most remarkable. Their construction is unbelievably fine. Some of them are so flimsy as to be almost unreal. It is the feathers which give the bird its shape. Imagine a bird without feathers and it looks very different. The skin of most animals encloses them and defines their shape but the feathers give the bird its characteristic shape. They also form a sort of halfway house to the air. We could say that the covering of a bird consists of feathers and air and we can observe how, on a cold day, the bird puffs its feathers out to enclose air and keep warm.

If we look at the way a bird eats, we see again what little relationship it has to the earth compared with other animals. When cows, cats or dogs eat, it looks as if they enjoy their food, but the bird has no teeth, no sense of smell, and, as far as we know, no sense of taste. It picks food up and immediately swallows it. It has a dry mouth, cannot savour its food by chewing it and has to rely on other organs completely for digestion. A bird has a sort of extra storehouse called a crop and the food has to be ground up there instead of chewed before it is swallowed properly. For that reason the bird often has to swallow bits of grit to act as grindstones. At the other end the digestive tract is very primitive. Solids and liquids are expelled together.

In common with the fishes, the bird does not carry its young inside itself but lays eggs. Whereas, however, the fish abandons them to mother nature, the bird sits on them to keep them warm so that they may hatch.

If we look at the structure of a bird we see that it has head, body and legs, but strangely out of proportion. The head is only an extension of the body and the legs are certainly not for running or jumping. They are just tiny supports for the body when it lands. One thing we notice very clearly. The eye of the bird is very much awake. A friendly robin may come and watch us in the garden and his eye is very alert. His head jerks from one position to another so that he spies any tit-bit that may appear. A sudden noise, however, will frighten him away.

It is true of all birds that they are very sensitive as to what is taking place around them, especially what can be seen and heard. We know that the eagle, the king of the birds, has extraordinary sight and can see the smallest animal from very high up.

We might say that the bird's speciality is its lungs; we could also say its wings but, by comparison with the human being, it has not got a head. In fact its head is just a projection of its body about as much as the snout if we were thinking of a dog. Its legs cannot compare with the human being's, neither can its digestive system, but it has sharp senses. In the human being, the chief sense organs are in the head. We can therefore compare the bird with the whole upper part of the human being. The arms have become wings. The bird is a flying lung but at the same time it perceives, so it is also a flying head.

There is another aspect. Men and women do something else in their heads besides seeing and hearing. They develop thoughts. We have an expression about thoughts soaring upwards. Of his skylark, Shelley says:

"And singing still dost soar, and soaring ever singest".

Thanks to the wonderful gift of feathers, the bird can soar. The human being has no feathers but his thoughts can soar to the heavens.

USEFUL POEMS

Unstooping, Walter de la Mare

Hiawatha's Brothers, Henry Wadsworth Longfellow

From Venus and Adonis (The Horse), William Shakespeare

The Elephant, Hilaire Belloc

The Elephant, Herbert Asquith

The Lamb, William Blake

The Tiger, William Blake

The Badgers, Eden Phillpotts

The Plaint of the Camel, Charles Edward Carryl

A Green Cornfield (Skylark), Christina Rossetti

The Eagle, Alfred, Lord Tennyson

To the Skylark, Percy Bysshe Shelley

To a Skylark, William Wordsworth

To the Cuckoo, William Wordsworth

The Green Linnet, William Wordsworth

Birds' Nests, Norman Ault

BIBLIOGRAPHY

In the preparation of these notes liberal reference has been made to the works of Rudolf Steiner which, however, cover too wide a spectrum to be listed here. Books by Rudolf Steiner on education include:

Human Values in Education

A Modern Art of Education

The Foundations of Human Experience (The Study of Man)

Practical Advice for Teachers

The Kingdom of Childhood

The Essentials of Education.

For study of The Human Being and the Animal World, *Man and Animal* and *The New Zoology* by Dr. H. Poppelbaum (unfortunately out-of-print) and the following booklets by Eugen Kolisko are strongly recommended:

Zoology for Everybody: 1. Zoology 2. Birds 3. Mammals 4. Protozoa 5. Coelenterates, Echinoderms 6. Tunicates, Molluscs 7. Insects 8. Amphibians and Reptiles

About the Author

Roy Wilkinson has been connected with the work of Rudolf Steiner for over 60 years. Born in Leicestershire, England, he was educated both locally and in Switzerland. He attended the Goetheanum School of Speech and Drama, receiving his certificate from Frau Dr. Steiner herself.

After working at an educational center, he made excursions into the fields of medicine (with Weleda) and agriculture, and eventually became a teacher. Over some forty years he taught in Steiner and State schools in England, Germany, and Switzerland. He has also taught children in need of special care.

Mr. Wilkinson has been active as an advisor to schools and lecturer on Rudolf Steiner education and Anthroposophy in many European countries, in South America as well as in English-speaking countries.

Another major contribution is the writing he has done over a period of more than twenty years. Wilkinson has produced introductory books on Rudolf Steiner education and its philosophical foundations. These and his curriculum guide booklets have been highly appreciated by teachers, parents, and those seeking answers to personal questions. A complete list of current editions is at the end of this volume.

BOOKS BY ROY WILKINSON

Questions and Answers on Rudolf Steiner Education
The Temperaments in Education
The Interpretation of Fairy Tales
The Curriculum of the Rudolf Steiner School
Commonsense Schooling

Wilkinson Waldorf Curriculum Series:

Teaching English
Teaching Mathematics
Teaching Physics and Chemistry
Teaching Geography
Teaching History I: *Ancient Civilizations, Greece, Rome*
Teaching History II: *Middle Ages, Renaissance to Second World War*
Old Testament Stories
Commentary on the Old Testament Stories
The Norse Stories and Their Significance
Teaching Practical Activities: *Farming, Gardening, Housebuilding*
The Human Being and the Animal World
Plant Study and Geology
Nutrition, Health, and Anthropology
Miscellany: *A Collection of Poems and Plays*
Plays for Puppets

The Origin and Development of Language
The Spiritual Basis of Rudolf Steiner Education
Rudolf Steiner: Aspects of His Spiritual World View

Anthroposophy vol. I: *Rudolf Steiner. Reincarnation and karma. The Spiritual Nature of the human being. The development of human consciousness.*

Anthroposophy vol. II: *Evolution of the world and humanity. Relationships between the living and the dead. Forces of evil. The modern path of initiation.*

Anthroposophy vol. III: *Life between death and rebirth. The spiritual hierarchies. The philosophical approach to the spirit. The mission of Christ.*